Closed for Repair II

by:
SandraKaye

SandraKaye

Gotham Books

30 N Gould St.
Ste. 20820, Sheridan, WY 82801
https://gothambooksinc.com/

Phone: 1 (307) 464-7800

© 2023 *SandraKaye* All rights reserved.

No part of this book may be reproduced, stored in a retrieval system, or transmitted by any means without the written permission of the author.

Published by Gotham Books (November 25, 2023)

ISBN: 979-8-88775-436-9 (P)
ISBN: 979-8-88775-437-6 (E)

Because of the dynamic nature of the Internet, any web addresses or links contained in this book may have changed since publication and may no longer be valid.

The views expressed in this work are solely those of the author and do not necessarily reflect the views of the publisher, and the publisher hereby disclaims any responsibility for them.

Table of Contents

Chapter 1 **Adam** 1

Chapter 2 **Barbara (Partner)** 13

Chapter 3 **Family Affairs** 16

Chapter 4 **Friends** 26

Chapter 5 **Intensity** 35

Chapter 6 **Lost Loves** 47

Chapter 7 **Nature's Beauty** 59

Chapter 8 **One Liners** 63

Chapter 9 **Shades of Sadness** 80

Chapter 10 **Suicide Clause** 110

Chapter 11 **Thoughts** 113

Chapter 1

Adam

Tough Love

Dear Son,
You and I,
we had a tough time today.
I know we'll have more,
but I hope they'll be
few and far between.
I cried for you today and
I cried with you today.
When you're old enough to read this
and better able to understand
why I did what I did, please...
remember one thing.
I never stopped loving you,
and I never will.
I walked into your room just now;
you were sleeping.

Oh, baby...how I ache for you
in this life.
If only I could keep you
young and innocent and
free from disappointments.
But you have to stand on your own,
and soon, too.
Please let me be what you need –
to help you grow and become a man –
but even more than that –
to help you become
a loving, kind, considerate person.

Be true to yourself.
but mostly...
love yourself.
That's something that's always
been hard for me.
I never learned to love myself –
but oh... how I love you.
And if I've been wrong
in the things I've taught you,
I'm sorry, son.
I can only confess to trying,
and I've always wanted to be
someone you could look up to.
Your respect for me means more than anything,
and if there ever comes a time when you feel
I deserve it, I thank you, son.

Begin to Grow

I know how much you want to be
where you belong, right here with me.
I've seen the hurt you try to hide.
I've watched your face spill tears not cried.

I wish my life was different now.
I wish you could be here somehow.
We can't get back the times we've had.
What's left behind remains so sad.

Within a world we'll never know,
the love of a son begins to grow.
But hurt I've done you now will cost
much more than time your childhood lost.

I hold your life within my heart.
Then comes the day we have to part.
You'll never see or feel the sorrow
that took my soul – left no tomorrow.

The ray of sunshine when you grin
gives my heart cause to hope again.
There's nothing more this love can say
whether or not you're allowed to stay.

I know you'll never feel the pain
that comes from having to again regain
the trust from you I've thrown away.
And hope the love you lost will return someday.

Closed for Repair

You scare me with questions you ask.
Yet answers hide – refuse the task.
I cannot say, I do not know;
the words won't come, release and flow.

I've loved you with these feelings strong.
I'd love to find that we will belong.
The time should come. Is it on its way?
So that we can again share our lives one day?

Memory Lane

I took a trip down
memory lane
and back at once
came our lives again.

We were so close
you and I;
bound together
with love so high.

We shared our secrets
and planned ahead.
The weekends free
with pleasures fed.

I miss the boy
who's become a man;
now lives his life
in another land.

Nostalgia street
I have come to know;
brings back the pain
and love I owe.

The days were short,
the years rushed by.
Now all I can do
is wonder why.

Closed for Repair

You're all grown now
and share your fun
with people your age
who love the sun.

I've had my thoughts
and dreams undone.
What once came easy
now leaves me numb.

Enjoy your live.
Live it and love it.
When you're my age
that time you'll covet.

My son, I've loved you
every day of your life
and longer.
I had hoped and
thought you could,
would make me stronger.

You were coming into your own
when I was still lost.
I was always lost.
I was always running.
I never came into my own.

I was too anxious for you to love me.
I seldom disciplined you.
I never taught you anything.
It was as if I was running for office
and you were a voter.

Closed for Repair

>My little blankie
>keeps me warm
>and it keeps me
>safe from harm.
>
>It makes me smile
>both day and night
>and helps me sleep
>and not feel fright.

Sustenance

These are the things that have sustained me:

My arms that carried you
My arms that hugged you

My lips that smiled at you
My lips that kissed you

My hands that held you
My hands that touched you

My heart that beat for you
My heart that ached for you

My eyes that cried for you
My eyes that saw your pain

These things took me through the days.

Closed for Repair

Each time my mind wanders back
into the past
the emotions so overwhelm me
that my throat swells shut.
I discovered I could so easily
conjure up your innocent face in my heart.
There are no second chances in life
and I punish myself daily
for wasting so much of
your life
and mine.

If I had just one wish, it would be
to go back to the night
you were conceived
and begin your life again.

You were (I was) too old
for you (me)
to repair the damage
that had been done
to your (my) heart.

Last Years

It saddens my heart to come to terms
with the fact that I missed
your last years.
You were approaching the end
of your young years
and quickly coming up
on the best times of your life.

Now, you are let loose upon this world
with no worries or fears
and your whole life is coming up,
quickly at times,
yet, you think as others:
that times will never pass quickly
enough for you.

Sometimes I only listened
with barely my ears.
I'd always assumed you'd
be around through the years.

I felt the day you were conceived
How special you would be.
Though others advised I give you up,
I knew you'd get more love from me.

Chapter 2

Barbara (Partner)

Ease the Pain

I promise this won't
break your heart.
A healing begins –
our souls now part.

Release the pain,
begin anew.
This is what
I want for you.

The hurt will ease.
I'll watch you now
and see your joy
will begin somehow.

Your heart will take on
a meaning without pain,
and you can begin
to love again.

You've always deserved
to receive what you share.
Now you will find
someone who'll really care.

I really did care for you,
but I couldn't show it.
The grief was too deep,
to let you know it.

The walls of my soul
were too debased.
And the damage too great
to ever be erased.

Come My Way

All the beauty and love
and the strength that you share;
All the kindness and wisdom
brings home to me that you care.

I never knew friends could/would
make the world so bright
until your love came my way
and turned my darkness to light.

If ever someone could earn all my trust,
your endurance of my faults
gave me pause – that I must
continue to discover
the love from within
and find truth in your eyes
that all is right once again.

Chapter 3

Family Affairs

Finding a Mother

I've finally found a mom
that I can call my own.
It was almost way too late
now that I'm fully grown.

Until I met you I didn't know
what it was like to
have a mother who truly cared.
Of all those I had for "mothers"
you were the only one
with whom I would have better fared.

My life was one big travelling show
as I moved from home to home.
Perhaps that's why I've always felt
the need to constantly roam.

I know that if you could have been
my own mother right from the start,
the love I could feel that you showered on me
would have been etched much sooner in my heart.

I always knew the emptiness in my life
could never possibly see the light.
Until I let you inside my heart
I had nearly given up the fight.

In recent years I've finally come full circle
realizing how much you mean to me.
Never in all the wishes I've made
would I have learned how loving life could be.

I have truly lived, loved and grown
when I've had you on and by my side.
So now I will always call you Mom
and I'll say it with much pride.

I hope you will accept these lines
with the love they're meant to convey.
I know that as long as I have you in my life,
you will always show me the way.

Thank you for your love.
I miss you every day of my life.

Your Gift

I thank you for the love you've shown.
I thank you for the gift you own
that's let me find a peace within
and helped me learn that I can win.

You've given me a love you shared
and let me know you really cared.
You had two daughters and three sons,
yet made me feel as if I were one.

It took so long for me to see
that you would share your love with me.
I've never known a love so kind;
it finally gave me peace of mind.

And I thank you for the disagreements few
without making me feel so small and blue.
You showed me that we could still have fun
as soon as the argument was done.

You never put me down for spite
and let me see you weren't always right.
If I'd had a Dad like you from the start;
I would have had a kinder heart.

My life would have been so much better then;
too bad I can't begin my life again.
But know my love for you is strong;
you'll be my Dad my whole life long.

Thank you from the bottom of my heart.

I miss you every day that goes by.

I miss you
telling me you
miss me
and love me
and wish we
were closer.
I miss the tiny
amount of time
that you were
my mom.

The luckiest day of my life was when I met you.
So sad that it was so late in coming. Such a shame.

I am so amazed how B and D seem to love me
unconditionally.
I never thought there would be anyone who did love me for
who I am.

Newlyweds

Tell me your dreams.
All that you desire.
I'll share with you, Love,
what sets my heart afire.

This day we come forth
to share what we know
of all lifes' treasures
and pleasures untold.

My wife will you be
my Love, my true calling
and husband of mine
you keep me from falling.

I could gaze into your eyes
all day long but that
wouldn't make them any less deep.
And when all is said and done
and the whole day is through
you have all the promises
I've made to keep.

You are the being
in the depths of my soul.
I know you will have me
when our love becomes whole.

So give all that you have
and all that you are.
When this day is through
we will have come so far.

SandraKaye

My heart's all aflutter;
my life is on hold.
from this day that we kiss,
together we'll grow old.

Sue

We came together as family though we were worlds apart.
And the love you bestowed certainly gave me quite a start.

You laughed at my jokes and you cried when I fell.
You made me realize that life wasn't all hell.

Although life has been hard; sometimes it seems, unfairly dealt,
you always had a smile; tried to see how I felt.

You tried to show me the power of positive thinking,
despite all the pain and despair when I felt I was sinking.

When my son came to me into a world unknown,
I knew with you there he would always be home.

No one apart from me ever loved him as much
as you when you held him; quieted him with your touch.

You've given so much to him – nurturing – which I lack
and helped him immensely to stay on the right track.

You've never failed to help me in some way or another
regardless of your disapproval of my bad habits as a mother.

I'm slowly becoming, I hope a person of whom you'd approve,
one whom you had dreamed of, but so often did I move

away from your disappointment and your "meddling" way.
But I surely should have realized you would unconditionally stay.

Now I've tried to remain focused in an effort to grow;
become one again with your family you'd be most happy to know.

And so in conclusion and without shame I will add
thanks so much for being there through the good and the bad.

Perhaps later than sooner life at last will seem fair.
Until that time does come, it really helps that you care.

My life now is short; the years have gone by.
His life's just begun and I have to cry

to see that I've wasted so much time in this hell;
never known how to love; perhaps just as well.

Because I couldn't become the mother he would need.
Now he'll grow in his life and with his children take heed.

Searching

You gave her life
but not much else.
She never had
a sense of self.
She'd gone in search
so many times
but all she found
wasn't worth a dime.
Her sadness grew;
she stayed on trial.
She hid her pain
behind her smile.
So now she laughs
and hides her fears.
She wonders what happened
to the passing years.
She gave new life
to a son so sweet
but obligations
she couldn't meet.
She destroyed him too
and took his rage;
displayed it – now
it's center stage.
So now the tears
flow fast and free.
You see that child
is really me.

Chapter 4

Friends

The Key to Love

I've said it to you lots of times
but not for quite a while.
I love you more than I did before;
it sneaks up by the mile.

We haven't had much time to think
about the way we are.
But I can tell you how I feel;
I've found my shining star.

The love I've saved for your sweet smile
is more than you will see;
but it's there, as big as love,
as only love can be.

When I look into your eyes,
the love I see comes out.
It makes me feel especially good
to know without a doubt

that I love you. I hope so much
my love will never end.
I don't need to hope; I know
you are my special friend.

These words were written just for you.
I love you way too much
to worry about our changing lives;
I know that I can touch

your sweet face and hands that hold
the key to love and hope.
As long as it stays where I can see,
I know that I can cope

with life.

Beyond the Surface

You don't know me.
You have known that I exist,
but you don't know who I am.

You have been a part
of my life, but you have
never gone beyond the surface
of my existence.

I have not offered to explain myself,
nor have you asked.
But now, when time
is getting short, I feel
that I must let you in
on my life;
below the surface.

So sit down and
I will tell you
all that I know
and all that I feel
and maybe,
just maybe,
you'll understand.

And then,
before I die,
you will know me
and who I am
and why I exist.
And I will have
accomplished my task.

Listen...

Friends for Eternity

I have a great deal of concern
for you and I care
for you more than I show.

I'm glad we're good friends
because your friendship
is something that
I cherish deeply,
and I hope we will
remain friends
for all eternity.

You are so good and kind,
not only to me,
but to everyone else,
and you have a uniqueness
about you that
makes you very loveable.

I love you very much.

So let's stay friends
forever
OK?

You are a beautiful person.

Shining Sun

I think you're really sweet;
you always have
a kind word for everyone.

And every time I see you
smile at me,
I know there's one place
where there will always be

a shining sun
shining on us
and helping us
love one another
and everyone else.

Dare to Admit

Because I dare to admit to you
what I have felt and
what I am feeling now,
I have opened myself up to
a lot of pain.
I have allowed myself to be
ridiculed or
accepted,
to be laughed at or
understood,
to be thought of as
lunatic or
brilliant,
to build dreams or
to destroy them.
Which do I dare choose?
Which do you dare choose?
For what you choose is
what I become.
If you dare to laugh at me,
I will go to pieces...
but if laughter is what you feel,
then laugh you must.
But please,
do it quietly.
I will be better able
to endure it.
But, if you accept me and
what I feel,
for what it's worth,
you will find it
to be worthwhile.

Not Worthy

I sometimes have trouble
believing that you really
love me when you say you do.

I don't understand how
you could or would when
I know deep down that
you shouldn't or couldn't.

I know I am not worthy
of your time,
of your thoughts,
of your love
and yet you insist and
persist and make me
sometimes want to pretend
and feel
that I am worthy.

I feel terribly guilty
for stealing your love and
making you think
I'm a good person.
Because I know I'm not.

Deep down inside I know
I am not worthy.
I'm not fit to breathe
the very air that
belongs to someone else.

Closed for Repair

I have no excuse for living.
Indeed, life would improve
for all around me
if I weren't.
But, being as useless as I am,
I am also a coward.
I wish for death, yet cannot
do it by my own hand.

And so, for right now,
I'll go on living
and pretending
that I am a positive factor
in your lives.

Playing the Game

I've tried to change so many times.
I'm tired of being just "me",
but every time I've tried to change,
I just begin to see

that I am me and you are you
and we just could not stay the same.
I know that what I did was wrong,
but still I played the game.

One day I was you for a while,
but I didn't like it when you cried.
So I gave it up for that time;
the "you" in "me" just died.

I played the part of my idol.
But still it wasn't me you saw.
Although I looked to see myself,
I had to make a law.

I told myself it's useless
to play this stupid, changing game.
I thought it out not very long,
so now I am the same.

I am me and
you are you and
that's the way it goes.

Chapter 5

Intensity

The Depth of Your Smile

The beauty and depth of your smile
when it radiates from within
brings thoughts enough to beguile
and a charm unblemished by sin.

Your eyes pick up the brightness
from the stars that shine so high.
I've no need to feel your lightness
all I know of you leaves reason to sigh.

Your skin glows with youthful fire
as though still only a child.
My heart wants only to aspire
to completing that which drives me wild.

I sense the nearness of your soul
though the moon has long since retired.
Upon me your passions take their toll
fulfilling all dreams I've desired.

I etch your beauty in my mind
knowing that just a thought returns
to start the pleasure in kind
of this wondrous passion that burns.

With the naked longing and fear
that continuously burns with its shame,
I look for you to be here;
still my heart with your power to tame.

Closed for Repair

As I gaze upon your beauty with awe,
your sensuousness and body delight.
With splendor and contentment I saw
your willingness to satisfy take flight.

I love you for what you can show me
as I look into your soul.
Forever your power will hold me;
give rise to the passion in whole.

Please do not turn from me as I touch
and hold you in such high esteem.
I feel your compassion so much;
ache to hold you in life as I dream.

If words could give praise to this feeling
that makes me want to love you as much as I could,
then perhaps you would someday be steeling
yourself to receive me as forever you should.

I promise I won't ever harm you
in thought, word or deed or with sorrow.
My purity of love will charm you;
make you content; never wanting tomorrow.

Touch Me

Please
Do not touch me
do not open
old wounds
old scars
not yet healed.

Please
When I ask you
not to touch me,
don't ignore me,
don't make light,
don't laugh,
don't question.
Just don't do it.

Please touch me.

Closed for Repair

You inspire me to write the words
my voice through speech cannot express.
The thoughts flow deep,
the eyes now weep;
I speak only under great duress.

My mind feels things my heart ignores,
but touches so deep down inside,
I hear these things,
my soul now sings;
Do you know how hard I've tried?

There is no internal compass
if you never had a mother.

It's very hard to love if you have never received loved.

Locked in a Cage

Behind my eyes
I see a fragmented prism
showing memories
of shattered dreams beyond repair,
while in my mind
the dreams return full scale
dashing the hopes and visions
from when I tried to care.

I hear the demons
returning to grab my soul,
my mind fills with voices
that never make a sound.
I scream for my life
but can only hear my terror,
reverberating from within,
driving me to the ground.

I smell the perfume of the
forgotten fragrances of a life that now
expels only sour scents of rage.
The aroma is intoxicating;
keeps me begging for more,
promising to keep me forever
a prisoner locked in its cage.

Closed for Repair

I feel arms embrace me
with the force of a thousand vises
and squeeze the breath
from my very soul.
This gives rise to the reasons
that I cannot feel warmth,
grasping tightly to hold me
and at last make me whole.

I speak with my mind
to a heart that has become mute
and silent in a world
that never shuts down.
Talking to a mind
that remains speechless,
not comprehending the voice
that speaks without a sound.

Now I see only darkness,
I hear only songs never sung,
I smell only days of yearning,
I feel only sadness,
I speak only the lies
that reside in my mind.

Senseless

This mind is broken and shredded into senseless fragments
That can no longer be distinguished from reality.
Sorry does not describe the regrets I have had
that keep me connected to the aches in my heart.

It's said that healing begins with the passage of time,
and that there's a reaction for every action,
but the ache in my soul will forever keep me tethered
to the shame and the wounds that reside within me.

Every day of this life, while conscious and cognizant,
I exist to accommodate this spirit so badly broken.
Without question, the thoughts and humility left
are kept forever mute so that they can guide me

in my silent moments. Yet reason never dwells long enough
to allow me the privilege of exorcising the demons
that have found permanent residence in my awareness.
I look to you, not for deliverance or acceptance

of myself, but to that of which I have so often been ignorant.
Because this, this that resides within me has been forever
etched in my soul; I know that now. I know I can never
be free of the nightmares that haunt my every waking
breath.

You can whip me with your looks of indifference and scorn,
but you can never do to me that which I do so well myself;
to batter myself to the point that no amount of empathy or
healing or time or concern will make a dent in the armor
I have encased myself within to prevent intrusion
from without. Nothing you say or do can release
the emptiness and the torment that guides my every
waking moment and my every sleepless night.

Closed for Repair

The nights and days
of frustrating ways
have settled in my mind.

My soul cries out,
It's not about
that which I left behind.

Deep in my heart
the hurt will start
and leave me all but blind.

Thoughts disjointed
mind still racing
can't seem now
to stop this pacing.
How much longer
will warp speed last
or disappear
yet haunt the past.

Warp Speed

Why, oh why will these thoughts
not leave my head?
They are crippling my mind
in intensity and beginning
to paralyze me.
I cannot go through an hour
without dates and events
permeating my
every waking moment
and pre-sleep (dozing) times also.
Can something not be done
to curtail this painful remembrance
of all things at all times of the day
and the night?
I cannot continue to function this way.
There's little time left before
I become a blathering idiot.
Can I check my brain at the door?
Why is it always at warp speed?
I get ideas,
get excited,
get manic,
plan everything out,
then get shot down
before I can start.

Love Unknown

I've been younger now
for much too long.
I need to grow;
learn to be strong.

There's so much pain
inside my heart.
This child in me
will not depart.

The love denied
when I was small
needs now to show
I will not fall.

I feel her pain.
It belongs to me.
It's been so long.
I cannot see.

Love once unknown
can never find
that which was lost;
forever blind.

I ache to touch
your soul as one;
become with me
that which you've done.

You made me love;
look toward the light.
But pain long felt
cannot take flight.

It's seared too deep
to come out now.
But day by day
it's learning how.

Chapter 6

Lost Loves

Quit pretending.
Quit lying.
All is not quiet
in the soul
of the heart.

I stopped breathing
and forgot to start again
when I last saw you.

first place –
a lifetime with me.
There's a scary thought.
losing hold
grip on reality
stranglehold
losing track
losing focus
losing sight of
overwhelming
underneath
defeated – lost
a drain on psyche profession
deserve guilt, punishment
don't keep hanging on
no motivation – all crap.

Hostage Heart

I am so very much afraid of people and
I am so tired of being so afraid.
The darkness cloaks itself once again in my heart.
The fear of people sends itself
directly to my soul.

You make me want to hide
from life itself and partake
in nothing of value.
Yet I can't allow my mind
to retreat while this child
holds my heart hostage.

These thoughts I cannot express
without finding them lost
in the innocence of a smile.
Ugliness can be so much more
than skin deep.
When will I finally acknowledge that
I am less than no one and everyone?

So much conflict within and
fear and loathing without.
I may as well give up, be gone.
Despair claims my mind once more,
depression banging on the door.
When the heart is shattered, it is hard to
find the good amid the chaos.

You own my soul,
my piece of mind
is yours forever in these dreams.
I sell myself;
your love I need
to keep me whole or so it seems.
I'm not alive
without you now
and though my love is true,
you shy away
and make me cry.
What, love? can I give you?

Closed for Repair

The night guards its secrets well.
By day the guilt,
the obsessions,
the distress is kept at bay.

No one suspects the thoughts
that come visiting in full bloom
or the despair that guides the psyche
when the mind is full of gloom.

Obsession,
Degradation
keep vigil at the door.

And when sunlight becomes moonlight,
the truth comes crashing through once more.

Caverns in the Heart

You think,
when you look in my eyes
you can see
beneath the surface
to the soul
of the past
that links me
to the present.

You believe you see
the essence of the being
that dwells within me.

Yet what you really see
is the emotion
that hides itself from me.

You cannot touch
what I cannot see,
neither can you see
what I cannot touch.

This soul that resides
in the dark corners of my mind
takes root in the silence
that keeps you
from hearing a sound,
for my cries echo only
in the deep caverns
that run through my heart.

Closed for Repair

I labor long to grasp
the emotions
that linger
just outside my reach.

I must find the strength
to take back
to take hold of
to take charge of
that which eludes me.

This heart will stay broken
for the rest of my life
I'll never be done with the people
who pass through it.
Spirits shook inside like
a small hot flame.

Mind broken, spirit battered.
Thoughts/shame unspoken.
Forever shame etched in the soul.
The wounds have not yet healed
with the passage of time.

I have lived my life in this world
Alone, silent, forgotten, unwanted.
From the beginning of my days
secretly, quietly, always...always taunted.

I find solace in the darkness
that constantly surrounds me.
Having found no pleasure in the light
still disparagingly astounds me.

No god ever existed in my world;
that position is too hard to fill.
Perhaps a lifetime of tortured dreams
has now taken over my will.

Closed for Repair

Is anyone out there?
Does anyone care?
What does it feel like to be
a loser all my life?
What it feels like to be
a loser all my life.

I'm doing life without parole.
Which means no escape from
these memories and thoughts.
They are toxic and debilitating and
paralyzing and agonizing.
I always feel as if I don't belong.
Memories just devastate me.

I have no life;
I have no love.
All I carry now are the
memories that will
sustain me and define me.

I've lived my life without hope.
I've lived my life without love.
But the memories live on with
regret,
remorse,
no reconciliation.

I have always been too afraid to scream
when I am terrified.
The fear of screaming is more than the terror
of what makes me want to scream.
Considering the phobias I have of bugs and such,
something must have happened as a child
that makes me so afraid to scream
that I keep whatever terror I feel inside of me.

So you're telling me, "I love you."?
You inspire me to write about
the things my heart seldom knows.
I bury them deep inside with doubt.
I never welcomed them with an open mind.
When the words I heard were "I love you,"
more often they weren't meant to be kind.

I know life delivers nothing but blows;
the words were a game – never true.
So when you tell me, "I love you," oh dear,
my heart swells and skips a beat.
It's been so hard to shed a tear.
I know never should heart and mind meet.

Chapter 7

Nature's Beauty

My Oregon

The sunless sky
brings back
the memories
of liquid sunshine
I carry from the past
years ago in...
My Oregon.

The quiet silence
of the drizzle
of the rain
sings a song of
contentment
as the days go by in...
My Oregon.

Then lights have to
be turned on
in mid-afternoon;
casting well fed shadows.
But they shed
a comfortable glow
just the same in...
My Oregon.

Catch the Leaves

Whispering through
the night
the wind
slows softly, quietly,
to a stop
and catches the leaves
in the calm of its hand.

Intoxicating Love

The sheets smelled
faintly of your scent
after you left this morning.

I breathed in the
intoxication of your love.

I remember how you looked
when we came together
(became) together as one.

Your breasts were soft,
yet became erect at my touch.
I kissed your softness,
softened your nipples;
hardened them again
with my tongue,
as you did mine.

Your sensuousness excites me
and your body delights me –
time after time.

When your hand brushes against mine,
the electricity that passes through
would dim the city –
and not only for a moment.
I lie back again –
on your pillow
just to drink in
the last aroma
before
I rise again
to begin a new day.

Chapter 8

One Liners

The darkness always looks back.

How do you mend the broken and shattered spirit of a child?

Could I take refuge in your heart?

I make it impossible to love me.

Guilt will be the thing
that will finally bury me.

Lost time.
Time lost.

Dead brain talking.

Lethal combinations.

Raging rationale.

Dangerous disclosures.

Illegitimate logic.

Evil incarnate.

Vulnerable heart.

Dead look of the living.
Living look of the dead.

Guilt and shame are like duct tape.
Believing it's finally removed,
the residue remains
long after you think it should be gone.

Ice water in the veins and
a mind devoid of thought.

perpetual betrayal
perpetual oblivion
perpetual nothingness
perpetual darkness

Don't dwell in the house of pain
knowing that it creates a strain.

My heart has so many contusions.
My life full of false illusions.

Waiting and begging for sleep to overtake my mind;
to rock me gently in its arms.

Carrying my baggage.
All set for an
endless guilt trip.

The pallor of the summer sun
sallow in its weakened state.

Helpless when guilt comes
crawling, knocking, calling.

No god exists in my world.

Closed for Repair

There is so much inside that
no one has ever seen
or touched
or reached

It is so much easier
to change your mind
than your heart.

If I die before I wake,
please don't despair for my sake.

I am so sorry for the wrongs I've done;
for the hurt I've caused.

I admit now, I couldn't outrun my demons.

Time to pack my baggage for the guilt trip.

I damaged your soul
with my damaged soul

Liquid sorrow – words of wisdom

Darkness is just a whisper away.

Closed for Repair

Background of a tortured heart
gave birth to a fractured mind.

Why do you bring up the memories
that cause such pain to my heart?

Because I have lost the ability to feel,
I now live vicariously through others.

Blisters that burn the soul.

I would not be a casualty of circumstances.
I should have been rescued much sooner.

Death by Suicide – Death takes its own life

I first lost myself in you and then us.

There are those who are alive, yet will never live.

The weariness and shades of sadness
that dwell in a chaotic mind.

I am so fucking lost without you.

My reality is your nightmare.
Your nightmare is my reality.

I cannot stand to touch myself.
Which explains why no one else can either.

I wish my brain would give me the silent treatment.

Your childhood isn't lost,
you just misplaced it.

Never lived up to my potential – what a wasted life

I didn't have a choice because
I never had a voice.

My mind still talks to you. My heart still looks for you.

Lost in this world.

What is the true Language of the Heart?

My heart turned cold – right before I met you.

Reality is thin.

I want to run, I want to hide
because this life in me has died.

When you passed by, the world dimmed a little.

I lost my soul.

We are a casualty of the mental state.

All the shadows disappear in the dark.

The sleep of grief

That scream was the sound
of a broken heart.

Chitter chatter in my head (brain)

Those who are well loved
love well.

All the stars in the universe combined
would not be a large enough vessel
to contain the guilt that I carry.

SandraKaye

I wasn't broken when I was born
but it didn't take long to become that way.

Infinite sadness stays inside the
boxes of shame and guilt

If we could start all over again
would you tell me when?

A broken heart can be mended
but a soul will be destroyed forever.

Bruises on the heart... that's why it's closed for repair.

Endless grief. Goes on and on
and never dissipates.

I trashed my own life –
my whole life.

Chapter 9

Shades of Sadness

Ordinary Life

This life so
ordinary
could have been more
extraordinary
had life not dealt
the blows
that came riddled
with doubts
that left no options,
that left no room
to fight.
I fight this depression
every day of my life.
How much longer
will it go on
before it
shames me
consumes me
annihilates me
entirely?

My heart finally broke
long before I met you.
It ended the chance
of giving love so true.
I couldn't love again
without the pain
taking my soul.
Even all of your love
couldn't make me whole.

Run life.
Ruin life.
I won't let you
do it to me again.

Closed for Repair

This heart is bent,
broken beyond repair,
though I've tried and tried
to pretend I care.

I can't stand this pain.
It goes to the very depth
and core of my being.
I have no friends here.

How did I ever (even)
get to this point?
Where did this life go so wrong
that I can no longer function
as a whole person?
At one time
I was so smart.
I could do anything, but now
I have nothing
I am nothing
I don't live,
I don't even exist anymore.
I just breathe someone else's air.
I care so much
and so little.

When the day breaks
darkness dims.
Tears surround my
foolish whims.
Death knocks softly
at the door.
Calls me gently;
wait no more.
When night's crawling
back to me,
I shrug my shoulders;
cannot flee.
This cold inside
burns my soul.
Can I destroy
the devil's role?

Lost days gone by.
Lost time does fly.

If you were never loved as a child, you can
search for it for the rest of your life
and never know it's even there
so you never find it.

Humor Me

Don't humor me when I seem so sad.
It's the beginning of the end for me.
I mask the fear with a smiling face;
wait for you to put me in my place.

Don't weep for me when I seem so happy.
It's the end of the beginning for me.
I cry the tears behind these sad eyes
as my breath now comes in wrenching sighs.

Don't laugh at me when I sit by your side.
Please wait 'til I'm gone; do it behind my back.
I couldn't bear to see the contempt you show.
Don't do it again; else I'll have to go.

Don't show the way when I'm so lost.
Just mark the trail with flare guns now.
Don't listen to me when I try to speak.
It only makes my voice seem weak.

It makes me so much sadder still.
Don't hide your eyes when I look at you.
I'm the only one who's allowed to do that anymore.
Don't give me hope when death is at the door.

Don't speak for me when my voice is silenced.

What You Did

You had no right to do what you did.
You threw me to the wolves.
Now...
I have to stay hidden
when thoughts come unbidden.
Decisions made in haste.
Oh... such a waste.
How could you do what you did?

You had no right to do what you did.
You lied when you said things would be fine.
Now ...
you'll have to save face
and do it with grace.
My manners are mild
yet my rage runs wild.
How could you do what you did?

You had no right to do what you did.
I can no longer say how I feel.
Now...
I cannot let it out.
You can't know what I'm about.
Disaster is near...
wish you were here.
How could you do what you did?

You had no right to do what you did.
You spew forth your rhetoric.
Now...
You tell me how life is so unfair.
But yet... you really do care.

I'm not supposed to believe
that me you would deceive.
How could you do what you did?

You had no right to do what you did.
I can't prepare for the rest of life.
Now...

I feel so lonely today.
There's no way to wish the sadness away.
You took my dignity
as you walked away in glee.
How could you do what you did?

You had no right to do what you did.
You allowed me no say in what my choices were.
Now...
you put me on restrictions.
You're full of contradictions.
You expect me to conform,
yet don't allow me to perform.
How could you do what you did?

Promises Kept

When you're not around I think of you all the time.
When you're here, I almost lose my mind
I feel something for you though I know not how.
What hides in my heart will never come out now.
Sometimes you make me laugh. Others I feel so blue.
Could it be that something has touched the soul of you?
Don't laugh at me when I speak of things so deep.
Do you really think of the promises you keep?
The dreams that come now are loves not meant to be.
Would you believe me when I tell you I'm sure you don't love me?
I used to write of love gone wrong. Mostly now I try not to think
I know this love is really strong. Is it you who made me sink?
Don't make light of what I say, yet please forget my face.
I never meant to feel this way; did I interfere and invade your space?
I cannot live with this pain – it was never meant to be.
So please find it in your heart to forgive, but don't displace me.
There's so much more I want to say –but fear takes hold of my tongue.
It's been so long since I felt this way –my love was once so young.

Remembrance

Thank you for the light –for the love of my life.
Thank you for the remembrance of me.

You gave me the strength
to establish my life.

I wanted so much to ease
the pain in your heart and please
the loneliness in you.

In certain respects it's true.
For the pain began to transcend.

You never believed it was real;
the pain, the hurt that I feel.

My life is a burden undone;
it releases the truth.

Please give me the strength
to protest my life
as a pun.

Nothingness

I am next to
nothingness.
Beside me
stands
emptiness.
Behind me
hides
loneliness.
Above me
floats
contemptuousness.
Below me
lies
wickedness.
Ahead of me
shines
hope.

Welcome to my world.
Won't you step inside my mind
to see and
feel all that exists
within these
devastating walls
that are none too kind.

A Clear View

Where in the world
do I go from here?
Standing on the mountain
the view is clear.
Watching from the shadows
as the sun goes down.
Should I step up to the
water and try to drown?
The clouds pass over
the willow tree;
leave a whisper of rain
that's calling me.
The time has now come.
I run with the tide
and heed all thoughts
controlled by suicide.
Please hear me out loud
thoughts truly I can't speak.
They call from my mind;
leave my spirit too weak.
Good-bye to my friend,
to my son, to my soul.
Try hard as I might,
I never once was whole.

Still Waters

With the mind spinning like a CD
$33^{1/3}$ would be a much better speed.

The thoughts could be filtered;
given time not to clash;
decide if they're worth all the worry
or can be dropped in a flash.

They never quit coming
whether awake or asleep,
but from the outside it appears
that still waters run deep.

It's so easy to pretend
that all is well without me,
while reaching far inside myself,
there's nothing but doubt within me.

Face the World

I know that so often now
I pretend very hard to be
the person who you think I am;
no tears or tendencies to flee.

I live inside a frightening world
where emotions take control.
Yet far beneath this happy face
Nothing is left of the soul.

You believe in me – I will not fail,
or so you seem to think.
But how often have you noticed
I'm afraid to float; I'll sink?

I cannot seem to conjure up
in my mind the smiles we've shared.
the pain of loss is much too great;
and, oh god, I am so scared.

I cannot face the world alone.
How long will I last? You wonder.
Amid the cries of anguish now
I hear nothing but the thunder.

You let me share my life with you;
tell you secrets that no one knows;
began to earn my trust within;
then walked away to stem the flows

of tears now falling one more time
For the loss of a love so deep.
And while I've given all of me I could,
you'll always have my love to keep.

For deep inside my mind I've found
this love is nothing more than delusion.
But oh, the strength it has given me
with its incredibly real illusion.

Now fear again regains its hold
on the life I've always known.
It twists the knife inside my heart
laughs now that once more I am alone.

Pledges to Keep

Darkness spreads its cloud over me
like a blanket warmed for sleep.
It engulfs the pain inside my head;
pledges it will always keep

the promises of yesterday.
Those times of dark despair;
I always knew they'd return again,
even though someone is there.

I looked and saw your face so pure
always smiling in my dreams.
I never thought the time would come
when life was not what it seems.

There was always room at your side
when depression called on me.
But I cannot tell you why it's back;
it just will not let me be.

I've cried and tried and given up.
I have not found the way.
I know that life was kinder to
those who chose to stay.

Despondency is my last name,
my middle name is fear.
No matter that I tried to hide,
you always held me near.

I feel all this sad depression
slipping deep into my heart.
I never thought the day would come
when it tried again to start.

I felt that life was better.
For once I really couldn't see
the tunnel of darkness straight ahead
that so enveloped me.

But now I'm afraid to open wide
the gates of fear within my soul.
Yet soon they will emerge again;
this terror takes its toll...
once more.

Blessed By Guilt

Despair now settles in my breast.
It leaves me with no time to rest.
Take all reason with it now.
Remove this furrow from my brow.

In its place bring back the one
who made me pause; I don't dare run
from life and love and all that's hope.
Give me, at least, the strength to cope.

No one ever sees the frown,
for I wear it upside down.
When I feel its presence near
I have to laugh in disguise
and in its place, stem the cries.

I always seem to feel that
I have to prove myself to you
before I can become a person in my own right.
Thus I suffer both day and night.

I look for your acceptance and
your guidance and your strength
to take up the slack.
But I should never have looked back.

For when I saw you turn away,
my heart dropped, yet tried to stay
outside the walls that I have built
made by shame and blessed by guilt.

SandraKaye

Your message comes through
loud and clear; oh, so true, what a fool
you'd have to be
to believe so much in me.

If I'd only been given half a chance,
I could have made your soul sing and dance
to the rhythm within.
Each of us has a place –
where things touch down deep.
You take the love – in its space
find a peace that you can keep.

I wanted to show you that I will succeed.
I was just hoping that you'd share my joy –
foolish me with my need. Your face would reflect
the hope in my eyes and you'd never
reject my faults – you're too wise.

You knew only too well – how often I fell;
tried to pretend things were right
while screaming deep into the night –
dreaming of lives
lost somewhere in time –
before full conception
of every deception.

Dreams are Never New

Anguish is knocking once again
invading all my dreams.
I see nothing; hear the sounds
of darkness filled with screams.

These dreams that come seem never new;
the only things I own.
I try to rid myself of them,
though their truth is all I've known.

The dreams that so invade my sleep;
not a sound am I allowed
to make to wake myself from fear
of crying right out loud.

I arise in darkened pre-dawn hours
with a terror I can't refute.
All that I remember now
is the fear that keeps me mute.

When I was young, a frightened child,
I kept fears deep inside.
I sensed that speaking aloud of them
would force me to run and hide.

You see, there was a time when I
thought my mother loved me so.
Yet when I told her I was scared,
she threatened to let me go.

So not a word would I expel,
she wouldn't hear my screams.
That must be why the fear's still here;
emerges only in my dreams.

This Heart That Bleeds

Could someone tell me, please,
could you maybe tell me how to ease
this pain that's inside my head
that so often makes me dread
this life I have always led?

And why do these have to be
so guilt ridden always in me?
I cannot seem to tame
this heart that bleeds with shame;
I've always been the one I blame.

Would a day without sorrow
or anguish for each tomorrow
feel guiltless and more exciting
than what's in me always fighting
if the pain was less inviting?

I cannot count these days so tough.
Eternity is not nearly time enough
to rid my mind of self-abuse and hate;
it's been there forever, keeping up this state
of self-loathing. I know it's too late.

Days have gone by and years have passed.
Farewell to the childhood that didn't last.
I've tried so hard; I'm tired now.
I know that time left me somehow,
so here I sit: I broke the vow.

Waking Hours

I told myself when my son was born,
he would never feel quite as forlorn
as I feel now and felt when young.
I learned quite fast to hold my tongue.
But the unspoken messages always stung.

His face I see all my waking hours.
This pain I've caused and kept in my heart sours.
Although deep within my mind I know
I'm not at fault; I can't let go,
the heart learns truth much too slow.

Despair seems to be a permanent feeling.
Always my companion, it keeps me reeling;
awake or in dreams these thoughts consume.
But the buried soul I cannot exhume,
its death is forever I must presume.

So these days will pass and life will end.
I fear I'll never begin or learn to mend.
I'll remain companion to guilt overpowering,
and face the truth that stands towering
over me. For all time it will keep me cowering.

Condemnation

I am so very sorry
for ending life this way.
Please do not condemn me
for what I have to say.

My life has been in turmoil
from things I can't control.
So now I need to end it.
Perhaps you'll save my soul.

I never tried to hurt you;
certainly not my son.
I loved him more than life itself,
now I admit – you've won.

The woman who has loved me
will never know the pain
I endured to keep my life intact
and discontinue all the shame.

The Human Spirit

More than anything in this life I want to feel love.
But even more than that, I want to feel loved.
So often I feel that life has passed me by.
I cannot seem to find the strength within my soul
to become the person I might otherwise be.

I have loved with a passion unsurpassed by mortal thoughts.
But I have never experienced the feeling of being loved.
When I have loved,
I have given my whole
body,
soul,
spirit,
mind.

I have always loved the wrong person,
for whatever the reasons might be.

I love you with an intensity that astonishes even me,
but I cannot pretend any longer.
I am so afraid to look at you because I know
you can see right through me.
I pretend to be a person untouched by the depths
of emotions that belong to the human spirit.
I cannot foresee a time in my life
when I will feel that someone very special
will ever actually love me.

I try so hard to be a person that someone could love,
that someone would love,
but I always seem to fall short of my goal.
When this feeling of love strikes,

it takes my very breath away
each and every time.
My heart seems to leap out of my chest
and begs to be noticed
by someone as special as you.

I feel as if I could write the most wonderful
poetic words that humankind has ever seen.
And yet, I know that I can never perceive the feeling
that would accompany
such a delight in the human spirit.

This life I have lived has not been good.
I have stumbled and fallen many more times
than I care to admit or would be able to count.
Yet, in my heart lies the hope
that the ultimate gift will not continually pass me by.
I look to you as a constant in this world of unknowns.
But I cannot see you through the haze that engulfs me.
You stay for now within my mind,
forever in my heart.

So recently I was sure that I could continue to love you
as though you had never affected me in any way.
I have tried for your love,
I have cried for your love,
and still it passes me by.

I wanted so much for you to love me.
I needed so much for you to love me.
But even more, I needed to feel that you love me.
You think that I write this to you because
you are such a special person.
You are correct.

Closed for Repair

I beg for your attention,
yet I continue to stand in mortal fear
with the knowledge that possibly you may
actually love me in your own special way.

I have tried so hard to ignore this pain.
I have tried so very hard to pretend
that you do not affect me
when your very presence
strikes an awakening in my soul.

You think that I idolize you.
Perhaps you are right.
More so, I believe that
I idolize your spirit
because it is so pure.

Dare to Sleep

I dare not sleep
because I dare not dream.
When you come to me in my dreams,
I see the completeness of your soul.
It reaches out to me,
but never can we touch.
For to touch
would be the end of your existence
deep within my mind.

I shed the tears you will never see.
And hide the pain so deeply etched within me.
My spirit died long ago.
It never had the chance to survive
the continual assaults thrust upon it.
It is so easy to think
that love skipped my heart.
But it is so much easier to pretend
I never had one to begin with.

You laugh at me. I know you do,
but I know also that you pretend not to
and that you pretend not to care.
I know you are angry with me.
I know you do not trust me.
I am afraid once again to trust you.
I know you mean no harm,
but you frighten me so.

I need your approval and acceptance so much.
I need you to know
that there is within me the child
who never grew up and never knew love.
And so often, that child comes out
and tries to cope with the adult world.

But more importantly,
you need to let this child come out to you
and teach her all that she is lacking.
It is a travesty of justice
to ignore the ache that resides so deep within.
The time has come to exorcise the ache.
To hold me and tell me
that I was not and am not
responsible for the ache inside of me.

Chapter 10

Suicide Clause

No Escape

I don't want to live inside of me.
The pain is much too great.
When I have to live inside myself,
there's never an escape.

The ache that lives inside my soul
is more than I can bear.
Oh, I wish this pain would let me die;
at least keep me unaware.

The only way to rid myself
of this mind so full of fear;
I need to rid this body too
of life so I cannot hear.

It seems the people to whom I turn
try so hard to relieve this ache.
But the things they find inside my head
are so often a mistake.

So now the time has come to face
the truth that cannot hide.
The life that so many cherish...
inside of me has died.

So I'll give it up for ever more;
the reality is now.
And when I'm gone, please don't forget,
you're better off somehow.

Quiet Sadness

Sadness keeps you quiet
inside your heart.
Impossible to love.
No reason to go on,
not wanted anywhere.

Inward she turns to the demons inside.
Not worthy of life,
not worthy of breath,
unwanted anywhere.

No reason to live.
Guilt never recedes from the mind
or the soul.
So much shame.
The pain I feel for the pain I see.
I am not worthy of anyone's time;
nor wanted anywhere.

Chapter 11

Thoughts

I give my life
for all who see.
I give my love.
What will you give me?

I give my soul
for you to hear.
I give myself
and hope I'll appear.

Why did they kill
my son?
Why did they kill
our sons?
They should understand
that war is bad
that death is worse;
that everything else
goes in between
except love.

It's kind of scary to think about death
and the end of the world.
If everyone except one person
were to die
and this person
buried everyone and then
she died,
no one would be left
to bury her/him.
What a bummer.

What it is Really Like to be Bipolar

I am incredibly brilliant yet
I cannot understand the simplest things.
                                      I am highly functioning yet
                            I feel as though I am falling apart.
I have times of absolute rapture yet
I suffer times of deep despair
sometimes within a matter of moments.
                        I have loved with such intensity that
                    I have literally felt my heart break yet
                        I have a rage deep within that
                        drives the passion of my emotions.
I am a contradiction of terms yet
I crave normalcy for I am an oxymoron.
                     I have a gift some people would envy yet
                             I am cursed for all eternity.
I have the genius within yet
abhor my own stupidity.
                              I enjoy life with a passion yet
                      wish for death to take me in its arms.
I have a razor sharp wit;
I am the funniest person alive yet
I am the saddest person you'll ever meet.
                           I am prepared for anything yet
                       panic when something happens.
I want to be loved with the passion I feel yet
I am loathe to touch and to be touched.
                    I praise myself on occasion yet
                           condemn myself daily.
I am the infant of days past yet
I feel as if I am the old woman of the future.
                           I am perfection itself yet
                       a slob of infinite proportions.

Equal Together

Now is the time
when all must come
together
and be equal
and be one and be free.
To survive,
to be alive.
To live life
and understand
as much as we can. To love
to be love
to be loved
with malice towards none.
To know what it's like
to just be able
to live.

Closed for Repair

LSD
trip
beautiful colors
no reality
truth is gone

Marijuana
get me high
stoned or loaded
keep me happy
make me a fool
not harmful

Heroin
tracks
blood cells gone
addiction

got to have it
no real life
fantasy trip
get it on

I love dope
because
it kills my brain

Marijuana
is good
not harmful
but stupid

Pills
reds
yellows
blues

                s   d
          r   o
      e   w
     p   n
   p   e
u   r
                           s

Is this life?

We had our chance. It was in our grasp;
like the skin of an asp. It was our last dance.

Let go of my heart.
Run far from it now.
You can make a new start;
give it all over somehow.

Give up on my love,
that which tethers you here.
But a friendly reminder
will vanquish your fear.

Sleep comes to those who dream;
to others invites escape...
from those who hear a different drum.

You think this is easy?
That I can just walk away
And move on with my life?

www.ingramcontent.com/pod-product-compliance
Lightning Source LLC
LaVergne TN
LVHW020444070526
838199LV00063B/4842